REJECTION

THE RULING SPIRIT

Fay Ellis Butler, R.N., PH. D.

PRESS

Rejection, The Ruling Spirit
by Fay Ellis Butler, R.N., PH. D.

Printed in the United States of America

ISBN 978-1-60647-224-8

Unless otherwise indicated, Bible quotations are taken from
The King James Version, Copyright © 1994 by Zondervan
Publishing Corp., and The New International Version.
Copyright © 1973 by Zondervan Publishing Corp.

Fourth Printing 2008
Revised 2008

www.xulonpress.com

Dedicated

To

John Louis Butler

My husband of 51 years

PREFACE

Inferiority, low self-esteem, insecurity, pride, hunger for power, covetousness, jealousy, envy, etc., are all variations of the same theme – the desire to be accepted, approved of and recognized. **'Acts of rejection'** *by one person or a group towards another person or group usually results in behaviors that mirror* **'rejection',** *more often negative than positive.*

While ministering all over the United States (including Alaska), the Caribbean, South America, Africa and the Philippines, I have observed one way or another that **'rejection'** *reigns. It maybe in the leader or the president of a voluntary association or political group who is too competitive and/or inflexible because of* **'rejection';** *or, the elderly church member or parent who has labored long and hard and feels forgotten, consequently becoming bitter or resentful; or the pastor with the 'Jim Jones spirit' with members who must honor him more than God; or the single mother, who is struggling to raise children alone, who acts and believes* *she is the only one 'going through'; or the abuse victim, who is so tormented by what has happened, that he/she feels somehow guilty for what has happen.*

*'**Rejection**' affects our lives, our relationships and our faith in subtle but powerful ways. '**Rejection**' can be the spark that ignites the struggle for success. But more often failure and despair are harvests of '**rejection**'. I felt an urgent need to explore the many facets of **REJECTION,** identify the problems and suggest some viable solutions.*

*After many lengthy discussions, ministering and praying with my husbands and some special friends, Mother Lee Van Zandt, Pastors James L. Lee, Evangelist John Gordon, Dr. Gwen Washington, I knew it was time to pen this short 'treatise' on **REJECTION, THE RULING SPIRIT.***

At the time of this revision and fourth printing, I appreciate my sister, Joy Ellis Walker and my daughter Jacqueline Butler Williams, who patiently spent many hours editing and offering suggestions. I must give credit to my grandson, VanDon Williams II and my daughter, Dr. Fay Maureen Butler for 'delivering me' from imminent computer disasters. Without the financial help of my son and my daughter-in-law, Pastors Eric and Cynthia Butler of Omaha, Nebraska, this would not have been possible.

Finally, this book has been written because I really want to please God and share the experience and insights that God has given to me. Consequently, this book has been written because of the great longing I have for people to love them-

selves and value themselves as persons with the capacity for excellence and greatness in many areas.

TABLE OF CONTENTS

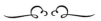

INTRODUCTION

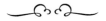

Rejection as the **'ruling spirit'** is pervasive, complex and multifaceted. **Rejection, the ruling spirit,** keeps working and manipulating until *'the spirit of rejection'* controls.

The definition of **rejection** clarifies the pervasiveness of this **'ruling spirit'.** The verb *'reject'* is defined in the dictionary in several ways:

1. To refuse to accept, recognize, or make use of or repudiate.
2. To refuse to consider or grant; deny.
3. To refuse affection or recognition to a person.

The word itself derives from *'re'* meaning *'back'* or *'away'* and *'jacere'*, from Latin, meaning *'to throw'*. Now consider giving in love your time, energy and affection to a cause and/ or a person and all or part of what you have given is ignored, diminished, or *'thrown back'*. At some point every individual has had some experience with **rejection.** This pervasive force, **'rejection',** does not always operate on a conscious level, where the individual is entirely aware of the reasons and origins of behavior, feelings or thoughts. Satan's conspiracy of evil is to mold man's thought life and behavior with the *'spirit of rejection'*. Therefore, the unseen war with **rejection** never ends until the end of time.

Rejection can be a specific act (or acts) towards an individual or a group; for example, exclusion from a club, fraternity, sorority or even a neighborhood. Obviously, there can be **acts of rejection, feelings of rejection, thoughts about specific rejection** and **behavior in response to acts of rejection.** The extremes become apparent when the *'spirit of rejection'* takes over the individual mentally, emotionally and spiritually and dictates behavior. For example, the worst extreme of the *'spirit of rejection'* is rejection of self manifested as suicide which knows no limitation as to race, class, looks or profession.

Understand clearly that the *'spirit of rejection'* is a specific demon spirit which desires to enter and dictate to any individual who has become overwhelmed by emotional and mental pain from **acts of rejection.** Demon spirits are constantly oppressing all individuals with the intention of entering, manipulating and or ruling the individual. Certainly we are warned.

"Finally, my brethren, be strong in the Lord, and in the POWER of his might. For we WRESTLE NOT AGAINST FLESH AND BLOOD, but against principalities, against powers, against the rulers of the darkness of this world, against spiritual wickedness in high places" (Ephesians 6:11-12).

In other words, we are God's warriors, ambassadors, servants in a real but unseen war – the spiritual realm. As I heard Derek Prince, a renown Bible teacher (now deceased), state that we are wrestling against real persons (the demons) without bodies. Therefore, if the *'spirit of rejection'* can overtake and enter a person's spirit and mind, this *'spirit'*, not the individual is controlling most of the person's behavior.

Rejection is also a personal experience that will oppress the individual intellectually and emotionally. Rejection can be felt, sometimes as inferiority, low-self-esteem, loneliness, isolation, insecurity, etc. These feelings can escalate to resentment, bitterness, anger, wrath, etc. Notice that if someone you care about or an organization you want join, or a neighborhood you want to move into, rejects you, it is pain — the closer the relationship, the greater the pain. A good example is the emotional pain of one or both parties in a divorce. Or, if **the rejection** is due to racial, ethnic, and religious bias, added to pain, are anger, frustration, resentment and possibly hatred. Further, **rejection** manifests itself in interpersonal relationships on all socioeconomic levels.

It will affect, not only the way a person feels about him or herself, but also how the person lives including the types of friends selected.

The poor, unemployed, the wealthy, the privileged, the famous, the unknown, Blacks and Whites all at sometime will experience **rejection.** Then, given the nature of the personality and personal culture, **rejection** may manifest itself in a wide range of possible behaviors from isolationism (the recluse) to rage, revenge, competitiveness, arrogance and negativism. It is noteworthy that King Solomon in the book of Proverbs warns the reader to protect his heart – the center of thought and desires.

> *"Keep thy heart with all diligence; for out of it are the issues of life" (Proverbs 4:23).*

The New Living Translation adds light to this important point; *"Above all else, guard your heart, for it affects everything you do" (Proverbs 4:23).* Since Satan is the **father of rejection** and will never cease, God has given the formula for protecting your heart — FORGIVE and FORGIVE and FORGIVE AGAIN and AGAIN. Forgiveness must be for others and oneself in order to prevent **rejection** from ruling the emotions and actions.

Understand that if experience molds and manipulates behavior, and so much of life's experience includes rejection, then understand the power and manipulative force of the *'spirit of rejection'* as well as the on-going operations of **REJECTION as the RULING SPIRIT**. To rule means:

1. To exercise control over; govern;
2. To <u>dominate by powerful influence</u>; to hold sway over.

Therefore, **Rejection** is not merely an intellectual experience in which an individual or group recognizes that they are unwanted but it is a total experience which affects the mind, emotions and memory. Even if it is a single episode, the feeling and the experience are imprinted in the mind. Over a lifetime, episodes of **rejection** may change behavior patterns and personality as well as health and well-being. One extreme example is the anorexic/ bulimic individual, who dislikes his/ her appearance and fears gaining weight. This is a '**rejection of self**' and '**self-hatred**' (inspired by *'the spirit of rejection'*). Note that anorexic individuals often die by starving themselves to death. Or, consider the abuse victim, plagued with guilt and self-condemnation, blames him/herself even though the horror was inflicted by another and/or others. Or, worst of all, is the child who is never nurtured or loved, but psychologically and/or physically abused, neglected and beaten may eventually become a sociopath and/or a psychopath.

Consider, also, that **rejection** can be a powerful force of motivation towards excellence. This suggests that the individual can conquer the negative effects of, for example, socioeconomic rejection with self-discipline and hard work. However, **rejection** can nevertheless **rule** the person that succeeds. Sometimes success (with the *'spirit of rejection'* being internalized) soon controls and may eventually destroy the individual. Some persons that make enormous amounts of money either cannot (because of the *'spirit of rejection'*) or will not because of extreme selfishness, spend money, not even on themselves.

My parents had a close family friend, who had a harsh existence, being abandoned at birth. She was a survivor. She worked at low paying jobs, saved enough money and started her own business. She fell in love and married a preacher who became unfaithful. This was more that she could bear, not having any biological family. She became very angry at her church because her husband was still permitted to minister the Gospel. Subsequently, she became more and more self-absorbed and self-centered. She bought one house and several others. At first she always had a wonderful car and was well dressed. She continued to accumulating money, having sold her houses and investing wisely during President Reagan's years of deregulation. Over her later years, she became a multimillionaire, and (full of rejection) she was still angry at the church and would not pay tithes. She only gave $2.00 per week in offerings. Her comment was that 'no one ever did anything for me, why should I do anything for anybody'. She even saved linens that were never picked up by customers but never used them or gave them away.

By the time she was in her seventies and eighties all she had was the house she lived in and the money she refused to spend – no children, no nieces and nephews, no friends, and no church family. The one thing that gave her confidence and security, her money, now controlled her. For example, if she purchased two donuts and coffee for breakfast, she would save one donut for lunch. She continued working well into her nineties. The only coat she wore was so tattered and dirty; her co-workers (not realizing she was a multimillionaire) took a collection and purchased her a new coat. Her statement consistently was 'no one ever did anything for me, and I am not leaving my money to anybody and I don't care if the State does get it'. Even though her experiences with life-long episodes of **rejection** motivated her to economic success, she could not forgive. Unforgiveness opened the doorway to *'the spirit of rejection'* which destroyed her.

Notice then, that **rejection** will come as long as there is life, but the will of man, especially with the Word and Love of God can prevent those acts and feelings from ruling man with the *'spirit of rejection'*.

Rejection, in addition to acts and feelings, is really an unseen force. Consider how heads of state and law enforcement agencies rule without citizens being aware of the fact that they are subject to the rule of law in society 24/7. Similarly, whether realized or not, Satan is ruling as 'prince of the world' 24/7. Because he hates ALL MEN, he relent-lessly works with **rejection, the ruling spirit.**

Furthermore, everyone who has not accepted Christ in the pardon of their sins is a servant of Sin. As sin's 'servant', the individual is subject to (without realizing it) the will of Satan. Satan is *'prince of this world' (John 14:30), 'ruler of darkness' (Ephesian6:12), 'prince of devils' (Matthew 12:24), 'prince of the power of the air' (Ephesians 2:2).* Since all are shaped in iniquity and born in sin, all will have the innate nature of selfishness and self-centeredness. That translates into everyone at some time in some way caused some measure of rejection toward someone else: the parent that disciplines a child more than he/she shows love or the parent that shows favoritism, the bully that harms a smaller child, the mother that keeps a man that is a molester of girls, etc., etc., etc. Satan rules all men who do not know God; he is *'full of wisdom'* (Ezekiel 28:12). He is working persis-tently to prevent men and women, boys and girls everywhere from repenting and surrendering to the Love of God.

On the other hand God is love. God is parental love, brotherly love, has sexual love, spiritual love, etc. Satan is the perverse opposite of God. Satan is hate, hatred within families, hatred between couples, sexual hatred (whether disclaiming normal sex or perpetrating abuse), ethnic hatred, religious, hatred of nations, etc. Hatred is a dynamic of rejection. One of the most effective satanic instruments, as 'prince of this world', is **REJECTION, REJECTION, and** more **REJECTION.**

SATAN, THE FATHER OF REJECTION

The complexities and permutations of **rejection** can be correctly understood only if explanations begin with the source, SATAN.

Satan was totally, eternally cast out of the Holy Mountain of God – **REJECTED,** when he rebelled against God. With his rejection he became, not only the "father of lies' but also '**the father of rejection'.**

"Thou art the anointed Cherub that covereth; and I have set thee so: thou was upon the holy mountain of God; thou hast walked up and down in the midst of the stones of fire. Thou was perfect in thy ways from the day that thou was created until iniquity was found in thee. By the multitude of thy merchandise they have filled the midst of thee with violence, and thou hast sinned; therefore, I WILL CAST THEE AS

PROFANE OUT OF THE MOUNTAIN OF GOD: and I will destroy thee, O covering cherub, from the midst of the stones of fire. THINE HEART WAS LIFTED UP BECAUSE OF THY BEAUTY, THOU HAS CORRUPTED THY WISDOM BECAUSE OF THY BRIGHTNESS; I will cast thee to the ground, I will lay thee before kings, that they may behold thee" (Ezekiel 28:14-17).

Satan's (Lucifer's) pride, self-deception and spiritual ignorance told him he was greater than God. Consequently he led this rebellion against God with one third of the heavenly host. (Remember God did not personally handle this rebellion; the 'archangel' Michael with other angels warred against the rebellion).

"And there was a war in heaven, Michael and his angels fought against the dragon, and the dragon and his angels fought back. But he WAS NOT STRONG ENOUGH, and they lost their place in heaven. The great dragon was hurled down – that ancient serpent called the devil or Satan, who leads the whole world astray. He was hurled to earth and his angels with him" (Revelations 12:7-9, NIV).

- Lucifer had awesome incomparable beauty; he was **REJECTED anyhow.**
- Lucifer had extensive political power and influence; he was **REJECTED anyhow.**
- His musical ability was limitless; he was **REJECTED anyhow.**
- He had supernatural wisdom; he was **REJECTED anyhow.**
- He had access to the Mountain of God; he was **REJECTED anyhow.**

Lucifer transgressed the rule of God. Neither his beauty, brilliance, political influence, nor musical gifts mattered. **Rejection** ruled. Lucifer, now Satan, still had supernatural wisdom which of course became corrupted. Bear in mind that when he became 'prince of this world', his pride and his rejection with his CORRUPTED WISDOM became the foundation for his demonic earthly manipulation of every individual who does not know The Lord as his Personal Savior. Satan is totally aware of how to use **the ruling spirit, rejection,** to manipulate the beautiful, the wealthy, the wise, the strong as well as the poor, weak, ignorant or uneducated because he had it ALL!

Therefore, PRIDE and RAGE, because of **rejection by God,** consumes Satan and Satan's armies of demons with the desire to defeat the purposes of God which is to bring all men back into fellowship with God – RECONCILIATION.

Satan hates God so much that his one aim is to devour and destroy God's most beloved creation, MAN. Satan has to go to hell but he desires, at all cost, to take everyone with him because HE HAS NO MORE TO LOSE because **he is already lost.**

Before any further discussion, bear in mind that Lucifer, one of God's angelic created beings, was in heaven with God. Lucifer's rebellion occurred at an unknown period in the timeless past. He saw and understood God's organization and hierarchy. With the wisdom he still has, Satan now imitates God. To understand how he imitates God, consider the hierarchy of God:

The FATHER, SON and The HOLY GHOST.
Archangels: Gabriel, Michael, etc.
Cherubim.
Other Warring Angels.
Messenger Angels.
Angels which encamp about all Believers.
Apostles, Prophets Evangelists, Pastors and Teachers.
All Believers (ambassadors for God).

With all his wisdom, Satan is not capable of being original and even has a TRINITY OF EVIL—**the beast, the false prophet and the Antichrist.** However, unlike God, **he is not everywhere all at the same time**. He has innumerable hosts of 'demons' and powers which he controls; they are regimented to take orders from him, carry out the orders and report back to him.

Satan.
The Beast, the False Prophet and the Antichrist.
'Princes' ruling vast territories, countries or groups.
'Rulers of Darkness of this World'.
Spiritual Wickedness in the heavenlies'.
'Ruling spirits over communities'.
'Ruling spirits in families' (generational curses).
'Demons' (familiar spirits) which 'follow' individuals.
Witches, Wizards, Sorcerers,
occult workers of very type'.
The unsaved.[1]

Satan's hatred of God and all men because of his **rejection,** marshals all forces of his evil organization to bring all men to eternal damnation – HELL.

Recall the Garden of Eden experience where Adam and Eve had perfect peace, perfect food, perfect environment, total dominion and continuous communication with God. Satan, in the form of a beautiful serpent, seduced Adam and Eve into disobeying the single commandment God gave them. Adam foolishly chose to abdicate all his greatness and submit to the serpent by eating from the forbidden tree – *"But*

---

[1] This is not a comprehensive list; it should suggest how diverse Satan's kingdom is.

of the tree of the knowledge of good and evil, thou shalt not eat of it..." (Genesis 2:27). Satan who had previously been rejected by God, wanted to get even with God. Remember, man was so precious to God that He formed man with His hands and breathed His supernatural breath into man to make him 'a living soul'.

When man willfully listened to the serpent instead of obeying God, God took His Spirit from man and put him out of the Garden. This willful surrender to satanic seduction caused all men for all time to be 'shaped in iniquity and conceived in sin' (Psalm 5l:5). Moreover, by yielding to Satan and disobeying God, man elevated Satan. Now Satan has become 'prince of this world'. He could now marshal his demons to limit, hinder, corrupt, block and stop men with legions of demons, especially, with **the ruling spirit, rejection.**

Note that after The Fall of man, 'spiritual genetics or DNA' dictate that every individual has inherited (from Satan) a sin nature. The sin nature includes the innate or natural ability to easily feel, experience and often accept **rejection.** Since **rejection** is part of the sin nature and is innate, many fail to recognize rejection for what it can become, a DEMON FORCE of destruction. Added to the complex picture of the normal sin nature is PRIDE which distorted even Satan's view of himself (no reality check) and precipitated his rebellion. Now of course Satan has become *"a king over ALL the* *children of pride"* (Job 41:34). One can therefore expect in most men that some level of pride will work with **rejection**.

"For all that is in the world, the lust of the flesh, the lust of the eyes and the pride of life, is not of the Father, but of the world" (1 John 2:16).

Isn't it amazing that this all began in the Garden when Satan in the form of a beautiful serpent, knowing the nature of mankind's independent thought (his will), tempted Eve so skillfully. Notice in Genesis 3:6 Eve saw that the fruit was good for food (*'the lust of the flesh'*) and was pleasing to the eye (*'the lust of the eyes'*) and was desirable for gaining wisdom (*'the pride of life'*). The *'pride of life'* represents the sum of self-centeredness and selfishness. Therefore, the 'pride of life' is always vulnerable to rejection. Individuals who are famous want more fame. Those who are rich want to be very rich. Those with power want more power. When efforts to attain certain goals fail, frustration and feelings of **rejection** usually follow. Satan, **REJECTED FOREVER,** persistently attempts to manipulate and control sinner and saint with **REJECTION** and deception, as well as pride.

God's love for man has never ceased or lessened. He made provision to again allow man to choose and offered man Life through His Son Jesus – RECONCILIATION and ATONEMENT or death through sin and obedience to Satan.

"For when we were yet without strength, in due time Christ died for the ungodly" (Romans 5:6)

"For by one man's disobedience many were made sinners, so by the obedience of one Man shall many be made righteous" (Romans 5:19).

"But now being made FREE from sin, and become servants to God, ye have your fruit unto holiness, and the end everlasting life" (Romans 6:22).

BIBLICAL 'SCENARIOS'
OF REJECTION

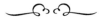

It is recorded numerous times in the Bible why and how Lucifer (Satan) was permanently and irrevocably **REJECTED BY GOD** and cast out of heaven FOREVER!

"How art thou fallen from heaven, O Lucifer, son of the morning! How are thou cut down to the ground, which didst weaken the nations!" (Isaiah 14:12).

"Thine heart was lifted up because of thy beauty, thou hast corrupted thy wisdom by reason of thy brightness: I will cast thee to the ground, I will lay thee before kings, that they may behold thee!" (Ezekiel 28:17).

"And He [Jesus] said unto them, I beheld Satan as lightning fall from heaven" (Luke 10:18)

"And there was a war in heaven: Michael and his angels fought against the dragon; and the dragon fought and his angels, and prevailed not; neither was their place found any more in heaven. And the great dragon was cast out, <u>that old serpent, called the Devil and Satan</u>, which deceiveth the whole world: <u>he was cast out into the earth, and his angels were cast out with him</u>" (Revelations 12:7-9).

The behavior of man, being 'shaped in iniquity' will inevitably in some manner mirror the behavior of Satan. It is normal to want and need love, acceptance, and respect. Everyone should have some measure of self-worth, but Satan is always attempting to pervert normal behavior. If you review the pattern of Lucifer's behavior, you will find a potential for the same in society at large – **pride > rebellion > rejection > resentment > bitterness,** etc.

Therefore, given the diversity of personality types, family culture and life experiences, the ripple effect of **rejection** will manifest itself according to individual's personality. Notice then that the permutations of **pride – rebellion — rejection—resentment—bitterness** will lead to innumerable outcomes of behavior such as:

Anger

Inferiority

Insecurity

Loneliness

Depression

Self-pity

Self-hatred

Suicide

Or perhaps

Exhibitionism

Extreme competitiveness

Inflexibility

Greed

Stubbornness

Extreme independence (maybe reclusive)

Arrogance

Hostility

Covetousness and envy

The Word of God, The Holy Bible, documents man's sinful behaviors: sins of the heart, sins of greed, sexual sins, and sins of rebellion in all the Dispensations studied in the Bible. The Bible thoroughly gives historical and supernaturally revealed accounts of man's sinful state and God's constraining long-suffering love with covenants and finally the Greatest Love of all, His Son. Throughout the ages and Biblical history, one can witness Satan's relentless war directly against man and indirectly against God. Generations following generations (in the same family) will be affected by the same malignity orchestrated by Satan with **rejection.**

Example # One
ISHMAEL

Externally Imposed Rejection
Rejection, The Ripple Effect —Generational Curses

Ishmael's mother, Hagar, the slave (handmaiden) of Sarah, used as chattel, was ordered to sleep with Abraham. Of this encounter Ishmael was born. This was not the birth resulting from a sexual union of love and respect; it was an affair of **rejection** (because Hagar's personhood was never considered). The order of Sarah (that Hagar sleeps with Abraham) demonstrated that she regarded this handmaiden as nothing more than a tool of convenience. In spite of this 'birth of rejection', Abraham was attached to Ishmael before the birth of Isaac (Genesis 17:18). Just imagine from Ishmael's early childhood until Isaac was born, he was probably told that he was the 'child of promise'. **Rejection** reared its ugly head again when Sarah ruthlessly insisted that Hagar and Ishmael had to go after Isaac was born. Oral history and written history are powerful. Ishmael's descendants (the Medianites of the Bible and the Arabs today) have never forgotten this **rejection.**

Satan knows that a child filled with enough anger and enough rejection will possibly be ruled by anger and rejection all of his life. Ishmael was filled with *'spirit of rejection'* and hostility at an early age, maybe as a preteen. *"He* [Ishmael] *will be a wild donkey of a man: his hand will be against everyone and everyone's hand against him and he will live in hostility towards all his brothers" (Genesis 16:12).*

Note that how **rejection** fathers 'the spirit of hostility' and self-defeating 'independence' even in 'generation after generation'. The Israeli-Arab Wars of the twentieth Century (1948 War of Independence, 1956 Sinai War, 1967 Sinai War, 1973 Yom Kippur War) found the Israelis severely outnumbered but each time Israel won. The Arab states –Syria, Lebanon Jordan, Iran, Egypt, Iraq, etc — were not very good at strategic planning. Divisiveness, competitiveness, greed and independence seems to keep the prophecy about Ishmael alive; *"his hand will be against everyone and everyone's hand against him"*. In spite of the fact that the descendants of Ishmael are in the blessing of Abraham, the strong culture of revenge, seemed to be self-defeating.

Example # Two
ESAU
Self-imposed Rejection
Rejected: Ignoring and Despising Family Tradition

Esau hungered for a bowl of red lentil beans and sold his birthright to Jacob. The birthright meant the first born would receive the majority of the family's inheritance. Moreover, Esau, seemingly willful, grieved his Father, Isaac and his mother, Rebekah by marrying two Hittite women. Jacob was already his mother's favorite. Knowing Esau had sold his birthright to Jacob, Rebekah probably sincerely believed Esau did not deserve Isaac's final blessing. Because Esau sold his birthright and was tricked out of his blessing, he was **rejected** as the head and future family patriarch (Genesis 27:37).

Esau eventually made peace with his brother, Jacob, who had deceived his father to receive Esau's blessing. In spite of this, the descendants of Esau, the Edomites (Idumeans) never forgot Jacob's duplicity. Subsequently, **revenge, malice, hatred, bitterness, resentment and wrath** were permanently etched in the hearts of the Edomites. Smug and secure in their mountain stronghold on Mt. Seir, the Edomites always sought revenge against the descendants of Jacob. Note that because of this strong unrelenting spirit of revenge, fathered by **rejection,** the Edomites for the sake of the descendants of Jacob had to be destroyed[2].

Example # Three
Jephthah,
Rejected by His Family

Jephthah was an illegitimate child of a harlot. His father, Gilead, had other sons who did not want Jephthah to share in the family's inheritance. He was forced to leave the only family he knew by his half brothers. He became a man of valor with great leadership ability and fled to the land of Tob. There he gathered 'outcasts' and formed a formidable small army of fighting men.

This was a time during the period of the judges when Israel was threatened by the Ammonites. Israelite elders asked Jephthah to help them defend themselves. Jephthah insisted on being made leader over Israel which the elders agreed to. When the Ammonites refused to negotiate with Jephthah, the Spirit of the Lord came upon Jephthah (Judges 11:29). This should have indicated to Jephthah that the Lord would be with him in battle. Yet he made an unnecessary vow to offer to the Lord, the first

---

[2] See Obadiah; Malachi 1:2-4.

thing that would come out of his home if the Lord would allow him the victory. Unfortunately, his only daughter was the first to come out of his home.

In the first place God did not require this vow of him. However, since the Lord's name could not be taken in vain, he had to give up his daughter; some think not as a human sacrifice but as a virgin dedicated to special service for the Lord.

Apparently, the feeling of **rejection** and insecurity was so powerful in Jephthah that he wanted extra insurance and reinforcement from God. He made a vow that God did not require. Presumably, he believed if he did not defeat the Ammonites he would be rejected by his family again. That would have been intolerable after receiving the promise of leadership over Israel, so he foolishly, although unknowingly, pledged his only child, his daughter, for sacrifice.

Example # Four
KING SAUL
Pride and Disobedience
Rejection by God

King Saul, Israel's first king, rejected the fundamental requirements of his kingship, which was to function within the law of God and heed the prophet of God, Samuel (who had anointed him for his kingly office) (I Samuel 13:13-14). Saul apparently forgot that he was appointed 'warrior-king' over God's people by God. He, presumptuously, offered the burnt and peace offering—the job God had assigned to His priest, Samuel (I Samuel 13:8). Then Saul disobeyed, ignored and rejected God's instructions from Samuel to destroy ALL of the Amalekites and ALL of their possessions and cattle. He saved King Agag's life and kept cattle.

God rejected Saul as king over Israel. When a man puts his designs and desires above the explicit orders of God, **he is a worshipper of self** (or an idolater). *"Rebellion is as the sin of witchcraft and stubbornness as idolatry" (I Samuel 15:23).* **Stubbornness** and **rebellion against God** is the same as **obedience** and **submission to Satan.** Disobedience opens the door of the soul (mind) and spirit to many other destructive forces. When man rejects the will of God (operating with *'the pride of life'*), he is open to the *'spirit of rejection'* and rebellion. He can therefore be manipulated by Satan. This *'spirit of rejection'* can foster ruthlessness, restlessness, obsessive behavior, mental torment, rage, etc.

Note that once the Spirit of God departed from Saul, *'the spirit of rejection'* in the form of a '**tormenting spirit**' took up residence in his soul. Saul's satanic possession was not abrupt or sudden but gradual because of his pride, self-deception (thinking he was more powerful than he really was), willfulness and disobedience. He could have humbled himself, confessed and repented for the first act of rebellion (doing the priestly sacrifice) and humbled himself before God and to the advice of Samuel. Pride and self-deception prevented him from surrendering to reality and recognizing his insufficiency. Unfortunately, he erased, blocked or destroyed all of God's favor for his descendants. None would ever be king.

Each act of disobedience, rejecting God's will, caused Saul more and more loss of God's favor. The *'spirit of rejection'* consumed him; he became so deranged he resorted to witchcraft – consulted with the Witch at Endor to talk with Samuel after Samuel's death.

There is such a thing as 'Divine Retribution'; *'Be not deceived, God is not mocked, whatsoever a man soweth, that shall he also reap"* (Galatians 6:7). Rejection by individuals and groups towards other individuals/groups, can be countered, opposed, challenged or even changed. But God, who is a God of justice and judgment, cannot be ignored or opposed. Sooner or later, judgment will rule because rebelling against God is rejecting His Sovereignty.

- Remember Achan disobeyed God's rule not to take any of certain possession for personal ownership. Because of Achan's disobedience (rebellion) and theft, God permitted a small force from Ai to defeat three thousand of Israel's fighting force while killing 36. Joshua, with God's direction, found that Achan actually stole precious items and had them in the family camp. Achan and his entire family were destroyed because of his disobedience. Achan was rejected by God and destroyed (Joshua 7:1-25).

- Nadab and Abihu, Aaron's eldest sons were destroyed by God' consuming fire, because they brought strange fire and lit the censers (the high priest's job). God was so angry at their arrogance and rebellion; He demanded the Aaron not mourned their deaths (Leviticus 10:1-6).

- Phinehas and Hophni were sons of Eli who perverted the law of God and the Tabernacle at Shiloh. They selected the choice cuts of sacrifice and did not burn the fat. They also slept with the women who served in the 'tent of meeting'. Because Eli did not stop the abomination and because the sons willfully continue their filth, the Lord rejected Eli and all his descendants from being priests (I Samuel 2:12-22).

Rejection, the ruling spirit, is as ancient as the fall of Lucifer from heaven. Satan, as the 'father of all lies' manages to use this ruling spirit through great powers of deception. Because of the sin nature (pride and self-centeredness) in all men prior to receiving Christ, individuals are always going to feel denied, abused, hurt and mistreated during different times in life. The further man moves away from God's moral, family and spiritual laws, the more Satan will reign with permutations of **rejection** because his desire is to rule in man's soul and spirit with the *'spirit of rejection'*.

THE RANGE OF REJECTION

One may think of **rejection** only as an act, an experience or a feeling. However, the satanic use of **rejection** and **'the range of rejection'** are almost limitless. **Rejection** can affect and/or destroy individuals, families, and entire societies psychologically, emotionally, educationally, politically, spiritually and/or socially. The variation and scope includes not only what is and was done to an individual or group, but also how the individual feels and responds.

All men in all societies experience **rejection.** However, different populations in different periods in history will suffer harsh extremes; for example, Native Americans in their own homeland, Black Americans taken from their homeland as slaves, the Jews (especially under Hitler, Goering, Goebbels and Himmler), the Etas of Japan who were of a pariah caste ranked beneath the warrior, farmer, artisan and merchant classes, the Untouchables of India, a large hereditary group that were strictly segregated, and permitted to do only menial labor. This rejection of the Untouchables was so extreme that everything they touched was defiled whether a person, food, clothing or furniture. The Aborigines, the original inhabitants of Australia were hunted, killed, severely segregated, prevented from using their own language and denied the right to raise their own children (who were placed in prison-like shelters), etc.

'**The range of rejection**' and the extremes of **rejection** could be understood by exploring the history of any one of many groups, including the history of many immigrant populations in the United States. One example among many is the experience of Americans of African descent that were brought to the United States under extreme circumstances to be sold like animals for free farm labor.

The Black Experience in the Americas

First of all, consider the power of written words — HISTORY. Written history is usually written by the victors with obvious bias. Therefore written history which may not be entirely factual will be treated as fact. Consequently, written history itself can be a tool of rejection. Even if truth is recorded but pertinent important facts excluded, history can still be a powerful tool of rejection.

Rejection is the refusal to acknowledge facts about a People...

The history of ancient Africa, Africa during the four centuries of the slave trade, colonial Africa, and Africa of this neocolonial period reads differently when written by Africans and/or Americans of African descent. The historical account, written mainly by Europeans, shows a vastly different and negative picture of Africa. That will obviously translate into negative opinions of the same populations which will tend to foster social, educational, political, racial and economic **rejection.**

However, the civilizations of the Nile Valley (one of which was Ancient Egypt) were dominated by people of mixed color (similar to the shades and variations found in American Blacks and Brazilians). In Ancient Egyptian paintings and the Tassali Rock Paintings of the Sahara Desert[3], the people were colored various shades of brown, black and a few white. Further, not just Neferiti, but Ra Nehesa and Takarka[4] and many others were Black Pharaohs. However, this reality was painful to colonizing populations. In fact one Egyptologist, Dr. Randall McIver, in 19th century England,

---

[3] Prior to 2500 BC, what we know as the Sahara Desert was all African Savannah grassland. Over grazing and agricultural practice precipitated desert-like conditions.

[4] II Kings 19:9; Isaiah 37:9.

call the age of the Pharaohs 'an astonishing epoch of Nigger domination' in the 19th century.[5]

Similarly, Ghana in West Africa had great Cities of commerce and opulence by the eighth century because of its gold. Sundiata in the 13th century and his grandson Mansa Musa in the 14th Century developed the Kingdom of Mali and the city of Timbuktu, one of the world's greatest centers of culture and trade.

The Kingdom of Songhai, which followed Mali, was destroyed by invading Arab armies from the east. With the invention of gunpowder in Europe and the invading Arab armies from the east seeking gold and slaves, the Sudan and most of West Africa was sorely weakened. By the time the New World was 'discovered', because of more advanced weapons of warfare, and the fragmentation of the Kingdom of Songhai, West Africa was ripe for dehumanization – THE ATLANTIC SLAVE TRADE.

Rejection is denying One's humanity...

Slavery is absolute and total **rejection.** Clearly it is not just the denial of freedom and forced labor, but also the denial of one's humanity. To justify slavery, Africans were determined to be less than human with no history and were called

---

[5] The Egyptian Sphinx is seen today without a nose because it was blasted off in the 19th century by Europeans — sculpted broad, more flat than pointed, it was decidedly Black African.

apes, cannibals and savages. Therefore it was 'the white man's burden' to civilize the Africans through slavery.

However, the West Africans were ideal for the labor required of them; they were already skilled farmers, iron workers, weavers and dyers and they could tolerate heat.[6] Paradoxically, the success strategies of the agricultural Africans in Africa were in part, the basis for their subjugation. The Europeans' stronger military might was the deciding factor.

Notice on the other hand, that there were African 'tribal groups' that could not be enslaved because their political and economic systems were based on hunting and warfare. Groups such as the Wakamba could not be enslaved. In fact they were so good at the tactics and strategy of guerilla warfare that they would hunt and destroy slavers. Food gathering populations (who were also very mobile) from Gabon, died in slavery as quickly as the original inhabitants (the native 'Indians') of Hispaniola (Haiti today).

The lie that 'negroes are naturally servile' coupled with laws that denied Blacks education, perpetrated cultural and intellectual **rejection** and fostered the idea that Blacks were lazy and dumb. Reinforcing these '**policies of rejection**' was the absence of honesty in the documentation of history. For example, few historians record how the polit-

---

[6] As early as the 16th century, the Spaniards discovered that the Indians of the Americas, who were hunters and gatherers, died quickly as farm laborers and miners.

ical rape of Africa laid broad foundations for generations of colonialism.[7]

The normal political and economic development of Africa by Africans was interrupted and permanently changed by the Slave Trade. That is not to say, that the Africans who remained in Africa were passive observers. By no means... The Slave Trade would have probably failed without the support of 'tribal groups' and coastal African Kingdoms. Thus, Slavery began what Kwame Nkrumah would eventually call 'the Balkanization of Africa'. For example, the Yoruba of Nigeria had 10 different groups. Instead of joining together against a common enemy, these small kingdoms with different languages were set one against another by slavers, who supplied them with arms and gunpowder.

Consequently, by the 17th century, the social, political and economic life of Africa in general and West Africa in particular was restructured to produce a steady flow of slaves. Free labor producing inexpensive raw materials facilitated the industrial revolution in Europe and the United States. Europeans and Americans introduced guns, gunpowder, dry goods and rum into Africa while developing vast manufacturing, trading centers and business communities in Europe and America.

---

[7] Read How Europe Underdeveloped Africa, by Walter Rodney.

Rejection is the refusal to recognize 'culture', 'history' and 'religion'. . .

The centuries of exploitation of Africa produced the big LIE, that Sub-Saharan Africans had no culture, no history, and no religion. Hollywood, the 'land of fiction and fable' perpetuated the idea of the violent ignorant savage through film. Negativity was the norm. Even elementary school books like, "Little Black Sambo" reinforced American racism. Notice that the ripple affect of this was to cause widespread 'low self esteem' and 'inferiority', a kind of 'rejection of self' among African Americans.

Not only was the history of the continent of Africa ignored but the story has yet to be told about the Atlantic Slave Crossing. No one speaks of the 55 successful mutinies between 1699 and 1845. The problem of mutinies was countered with the practice of mixing Africans of different language groups to prevent further mutinies. The inability to communicate efficiently further created far reaching social and cultural disabilities: the loss of vast amounts of history that had been passed on in the oral tradition, the inability to organize iron working, weaving, cloth dyeing guilds; the inability to organize self-help groups: the inability to continue many of the cultural traditions learned in the motherland.

The Middle Passage, crossing the Atlantic, was not very different from the holocaust of Nazi Germany. Those who were sick were clubbed to death and thrown overboard. On one ship as many as two thirds died regardless of what was done. The horror of the slave ship was so great, that given a chance, many committed suicide. Many refused to eat in order to die. Women were 'fair game' to the ship's crewmen. Men and women were packed in the holds and chained together (which was a social taboo). 'Culture shock' called 'fixed melancholy' caused the death of many slaves, even when the sanitary and dietary conditions were good. Remember all societies have fixed taboos (behavior prescribed and proscribed by tradition) which were completely violated by the conditions of the Trans-Atlantic 'Slave Passage'.

Voyages could be as short as three weeks or as long as three months. A few slavers forced slaves to remain chained in the filth of human waste during the entire voyage – the longer the time, the more deaths. Note that only one of two of the 30 to 60 million Africans kidnapped from their homeland alive lived for sale in the Americas to experience the further horrors of enslavement. Those who lived had to be severely affected psychologically, emotionally and spiritually.

There are many specialties in the twenty-first centuries which deal with post traumatic stress. Post- traumatic stress is not unique to war time or to veterans of war. Just imagine how, by the time the Africans reached the shores of the Americas, separated from families, sold to distant plantations, viciously subjugated, whipped, raped, chained, treated as thought they had no culture, religion or ability and then placed with others speaking different languages but in the same condition. They had to have suffered on-going post traumatic stress that has been passed on from generation to generation. *'The spirit of rejection'* had to have taken root in the souls of Black Folk.

Rejection is the 'refusal to consider political and economic injustice...'

Slaves were wealth producing property to the slave owners. The United States economic and political success was rooted in the enslavement of Blacks as well as the dismantling and disruption of Native American culture and political systems. The constitutional convention of 1787 was not concerned with the inalienable rights of all Americans, but only of 'White Americans with property' which included slave ownership.

- In Article One, Section Two, slaves (for taxation purposes) were three fifths of a human being.
- Article One, Section Nine stated Federal authorities could not interfere with the Atlantic Slave Trade for 20 years.
- Article Four of the constitution mandated that all fugitive slaves had to be returned to their rightful owners.

From the birth of this country, a constitutional democracy, the slaves were **rejected** as persons having inalienable rights of any kind. William Penn, a Quaker, the religious founder of Pennsylvania owned slaves; even George Washington, the 'Father' of this country was a slaveholder. Between 1792 and 1807, free Blacks could not vote in Kentucky, Ohio and New Jersey. Americans of African descent could vote if they owned $250.00 worth of property; there were no restrictions for Whites.

After the slaves were 'freed', they continued as 'de facto' slaves to plantation owners. The majority of slaves were unskilled farm laborers and to survive they had to farm as sharecroppers or tenant farmers. As such the ex-slave had to pay as much as half his crop to the plantation owner, buy the owner's seed and sell his half to the plantation owner. Any complaints would result in eviction or an untimely death.

Racism and violence continued past the post-reconstruction era. The daily and weekly newspapers and periodicals of southern cities, particularly in states like Alabama, Georgia and Mississippi had headlines praising lynching mobs.

World War I opened some industrial jobs to Blacks in the North and the great northern migrations of Southern Blacks began. The New Deal era under President F.D. Roosevelt helped the plight of Blacks. During the depression over 50% of White America was out of work; Home Relief (welfare), Social Security and jobs were created. Blacks were included. World War II further improved the standard of living of Black Americans because of the war jobs.

Rejection has been so pervasive and continuous that it seems that the chances for the majority Americans of African descent to become part of mainstream America seem to be decreasing with time. Consider the following which is common knowledge but rarely publicly addressed with plans for resolution or reparation.

- The increasing segregation of neighborhoods and schools, particularly in large cities.
- College enrollment of Black Americans as compared to White Americans, Asians and Latinos is proportionately decreasing. Miseducation and inferior education continues to be more marked among Americans of color. Remember eugenics was accepted in the United States among scientists and scholars as late as 1972.[8] Eugenics taught and attempted to prove Blacks in particular (as well as other minorities) were intellectually inferior to whites[9].
- Unemployment rates among Black males is disproportionately higher that any cohort.
- European and Asian immigrants have easier access to 'open doors' and lending institutions, giving them

---

[8] For further information, read American Eugenics: Race, Queer Anatomy, and the Science of Nationalism, by Nancy Ordover, (Minneapolis, Minn.: Univ. of Minnesota Press, 2003).

[9] In Queens College of the City of New York, there were professors yet teaching eugenic as a legitimate science in the 1970s. In the early part of the 20th century the Carnegie Foundation and the Rockefeller Foundation supported eugenics research. Theodore Roosevelt, Woodrow Wilson, and Winston Churchill supported this theory as well as Alexander Graham Bell, female activist Margaret Sanger and George Bernard Shaw. The list could go on. The crème d' la crème of American educators and politicians believed in eugenics.

economic success that Black Americans have never had.

• It is an unspoken and acted upon maxim that Blacks are guilty until proven innocent. The inequities in the criminal justice system are rampant. In fact there are just as many Black males in prison (over one million) as are enrolled in colleges and universities.

Marable Manning, a contemporary African American historian, wrote in <u>How Capitalism Underdeveloped Black America</u> that as soon as a Black child enters public school, the educational pedagogy rests on the assumption of the child's cultural and intellectual inferiority. He further writes that the esthetic and popular culture of racist societies making Anglo-Saxon culture ideal create the tragic and destructive phenomena of **self-hatred** and **cultural genocide.**[10]

Even though **rejection** is one of the powerful ruling demons and no person is totally free of **rejection,** Americans of African descent continue to be assaulted by armies of destructive demons marshaled by the **ruling spirit, rejection** in addition to the 'permanent post-traumatic stress'.

Satan's goal is to have as many individuals as possible being manipulated and or controlled by *'the spirit of rejection'.* Never forget, from the unknown past until now the fallen angels (now demons) cast into the earth with Lucifer

---

[10] <u>How Capitalism Underdeveloped Black America</u>, 1983, pp8,9.

(now Satan), have not stopped working, have not died with any person, nor have they disappeared.

Therefore, Satan maximizes as much sin and negative behavior in humans as possible by assigning special demons to individuals, groups or nations. Notice the harsh reality of slavery – kidnapping, rape, physical and sexual abuse, the forced separation of families, etc. – were acts of hatred, aggression and rejection against Africans. Remember, the residue of any kind of abuse remain in the victims conscious and/or unconscious memory. If the abuse is a repeated enough or the residue of abuse is not rendered ineffective through prayer and counseling, behavior will be affected. A 'demon' will keep manipulating thought and/or behavior until it is in control. In other words, **'rejection the ruling spirit'** keeps working and manipulating experience and thought until **'the spirit of rejection'** is controlling the individual. The following lists although not comprehensive, indicate part of the process.

Acts of Rejection

Physical abuse
(beginning, in case of Black America, with slavery)
Psychological and intellectual abuse (miseducation)
Sexual abuse (rape, incest, sodomy,
during slavery and in prisons)
Segregation, racism and discrimination

Media misrepresentation (movies and crime reporting)
Denial of moving to certain neighborhoods
Denial of economic access
(Business loans, skilled jobs, mortgages).

Feelings from Rejection

Inferiority, Low self-esteem
Self-hatred, loneliness.
Self pity, suicide.
Anger, rage, wrath
Resentment, bitterness, rebellion
Hatred and Murder
Jealousy, envy, covetousness

Results of Personal Rejection

Extreme independence and willfulness.
Withdrawal and becoming reclusive.
Pride, arrogance, greed.
Compulsive violent behavior, possessiveness
Fear of failure and Fear of the future
Intimidation and a drawback spirit
Unclean thoughts and desires
Tormenting dreams[11]

---

[11] The last two on the list are especially true for the sexually abused.

The plan of Satan is to control as many as he can with a *'spirit of rejection'* and he is working at this 24/7. This *'spirit of rejection'* can be passed down from generation to generation and will be strengthened by selfishness, self-centeredness, self-pity in individuals as well as conflict and disunity in families.

However, even though the Black experience in America has been a non-ending crisis[12], Blacks have endured and survived in spite of the permutations of rejection in the political, economic, social and health arenas. The strength of the Black Family and the Black Church (as family and as community) has caused success for many individuals and families. There is a lot of joblessness, dysfunction and frustration, but somehow even with the obvious and not so obvious rejection, the Power and blessings of God are available. Therefore those who God blesses, no matter what the circumstances, no one can curse.

---

[12] The incremental effects of drugs and alcohol are not discussed here because an entire book could be written. It must be added that the intentional introduction of controlled substances in Black communities is part of the African American Heritage in the United States.

THE PERSONAL SCENARIO
OF REJECTION

Although the above chapters deal with Biblical and broad historical and societal themes relating to **rejection as a ruling spirit,** there are numerous ways individuals are affected by **rejection,** particularly in the 21st century. Remember, demons and demonic behavior can be transferred to descending generations. Satan's evil does NOT die with individuals; it is passed down TO DESCENDING GENERATIONS. Some call these demonic assignments 'generational curses'. Included in this are incest, alcoholism, drug addiction, murder, greed, and stealing that plague specific families. These behaviors derive, not only from imitation, but also from demonic transference from generation to generation.

"And the Lord passed by before him, and proclaimed,
The Lord, The Lord God, Merciful and gracious,

longsuffering, and abundant in goodness and truth, keeping mercy for thousands, forgiving iniquity and transgressions and sin, and that will by no means clear the guilty; visiting the iniquity of the fathers upon the children, and upon the children's children, unto the third and to the fourth generation" (Genesis 34:7).[13]

Even though we are under Grace and Jesus has come with forgiveness, the principles of 'generational curses' hold true to those who have not committed their lives to Christ. Satan, as the 'prince of this world' and the 'prince of the powers of the air', is free to work the same successful evil in any family generation after generation which allows themselves to be vulnerable.

However, on the personal level, **rejection** works within the 'inner man' in the form of *'the spirit of rejection'* so that an individual may reject much of what is good about him/herself, as well as distrust and reject the help of others. Further, **rejection** may work in insidiously subtle ways within one own social group; the family, the church, the club, etc. The closer the relationship, the more painful are the **'acts of rejection'.** Consider that if someone in Lapland, Greenland or Iceland, tells you that you are unwanted and disliked, it would not cause an extra blink of the eyelids. You are not interested in being in those countries or knowing the

[13] See also Exodus 20:5; Num.14:28; II Chron.19:1-11).

inhabitants. However, if your family members, for example, in the city in which all of you reside had a family gathering and did not invite you, you would be devastated and want to know why. The act of ignoring you is **rejection** and the emotional pain is also **rejection.**

Consider the strong feelings of rejection and loneliness that almost always consume adopted children by the age of 12 or 13 years. Regardless of how much love, training and attention an adopted child has been given, the belief that their biological parents did not want him/her preoccupies the thoughts so much that rejection invades the mind and emotions, thus leading to resentment, hostility and rebellion. The child and many times the adoptive parents are not aware of a strong *'spirit of rejection'* ruling the child. By the time the child wants to run away to find his/her biological parents, a lifetime of love and nurturing is not powerful enough to stop the child.

Further there are various **'acts of rejection'** occurring in families everyday. For example, all too often, preferential treatment will be given to one child over another because of gender, age, or even physical appearance. It doesn't help when the parents rationalize by saying 'he's the oldest' or 'she's the baby'. Preferential treatment of one child results in **rejection** of other siblings. If this continues, feelings of **rejection, insecurity,** and **inferiority** begin to rule in the emotions and eventually in the behavior of the other children.

Case # One
Family Style Rejection

This woman has been married twice, and both husbands treated her horribly, partly because of her own submissiveness. **Seeking for love, she became 'a doormat'** for both husbands. She was looking for the love and understanding she had never received in her childhood. She came from a home in which both parents worked hard everyday and were home every night. She was well fed, well clothed, graduated from high school and attended church.

However, in her home, no one ever encouraged her academically, nor was she ever told she looked good. There was rarely any family communication and enjoyment. In fact, she visited the homes of her neighbor to enjoy a family atmosphere of love and warmth. When she started developing physically with a voluptuous figure, she was accused of being 'fresh'. Because she learned to be passive, she was fondled by men (uncles and cousins) in her family but she was afraid to tell her mother. To her she could never do anything right.

One would have to look at her parents' background to realize, neither of the parents had adequate nurturing, love or encouragement. Therefore, **'rejection'** was part of the family's social DNA. Her mother was a child born out of wedlock, who looked different from her siblings and was unfairly treated all of her childhood. In fact, she was 12 years old before her mother allowed her to start school while all her younger siblings started in first grade. She, in effect, was hidden from society for twelve years doing most of the house work and cooking.

The above young woman's father was orphaned as a very young lad. Having a very small family, he had to fend for himself since he was very young. He had no protection or nurturing but was a hard working survivor. These two parents with histories of **rejection** married one another but could not show love to one another or to their children because they had never experienced love from nurturing parents. They were both excellent providers but not nurturers. Their daughter, who now has children and grandchildren, is still battling the self-destructive effects of childhood **rejection.**

Low self-esteem and unworthiness (fathered by **rejection**) was not intentionally passed on to this daughter by her parents but it was part of the family culture. In the lives of both parents there was more **rejection** than love and more discipline than encouragement (very little gaiety and good times). The daughter's **rejection** created emotional problems because she began to look for both husbands to give

her the impossible; the love, nurturing, encouragement and support that her parents never had given
her in childhood.[14] The daughter went to the excess
in being maid, cook, lover, everything ('a doormat')
which brought out the worst in her husbands —
exploitation, meanness and infidelity. All this caused
more painful **rejection.**

Rejection and its effects multiply when individuals
have been sexually abused whether incest, rape, sodomy or
fondling. Part of the power of **the ruling spirit of rejection,**
is that deception is always there. Since Satan's demons never
work alone, 'lying demons' will accompany **rejection** – self
accusation, guilt, insanity demons, etc. In addition to all the
post traumatic effects, after, is the overwhelming shame and
guilt. Guilt smothering innocence is one of the best exam-
ples demonstrating Satan's maliciousness. Guilt is a 'demon'
which makes the individual feel responsible for sin and filth
even when that individual is not guilty.

Reflect and remember that Satan was around when God
created man and made provision for man to have healthy
moral and righteous relationships.

---

[14] All too often, spouses are struggling with their own 'rejection'. It
is consummately unfair to expect, the spouse to be father, mother and
spouse.

"Therefore shall a man leave his father and his mother and shall cleave to his wife: and they shall be one flesh" (Genesis 2:24).

The one thing Satan is relentless about is polluting sexual and social relationships. The younger and younger Satan can afflict his sexual and social pollution on individuals, the more time he has to work on destroying their outlook on life and themselves.

Sexual abuse and extreme physical abuse, even if a one time event, has layers of **rejection** associated with and following the single episode. Added to the mental and emotional trauma, is the physical abuse from the forceful trauma. In fact, some women will have recurring pain in the vaginal area for years when there is no evidence of pathology. Abuse of any kind is never an isolated final act. **Rejection** lives on in the memory and emotions. Furthermore, with rape in particular, Satan is determined to make that horrible episode of rejection live on with NIGHTMARES and other types of real fear.

Satan of course, is not going to inform the victim that the residue of the abuser's filth, a **lust spirit,** may follow the victim. This 'lust spirit' becomes a magnet for other sexually sick individuals to further attempt to abuse the same victim. Of course, the guilt will further torment the individual who never realizes that Satan and the entire 'residue' from the initial abuse are manipulating their life.

Rejection affects the rich, the poor, the famous, the homeless, and persons of every ethnicity and race. Satan hates everyone. As sad as it is, one wonders why individuals like Marilyn Monroe and Judy Garland, both famous, rich, talented and beautiful, committed suicide. The only answer can be *'the spirit of rejection'* ruled so powerfully, that they did not want to live. Both were 'objects' to be marketed, one as a sex object and the other as an entertainment 'money making machine'. When it came to their emotions and what they really needed or wanted, they were 'personas non gratis'.

At the other end of the spectrum were two 'nightmare personalities' who were determined to be something because they were made to feel like nothing – Hitler and Stalin. Hitler had an abusive lonely childhood with his mother. He was Austrian and not German and had a Jewish grandfather on his mother's side. He had a checkered, rejected childhood, religious and military career. His life experience made him a psychopathic monster determined to control the world. Stalin similarly was a child abuse victim who was been so horribly beaten by his father on one occasion that he was unconscious for days. He was short, homely and psychopathically determined to rule. He even killed his mentor Lenin. Similar to Hitler's non-German origins, Stalin was not Russian but Georgian. **Rejection** propelled them both into monstrous behavior and abuse. It is apparent that not only *'the spirit of rejection'* ruled them but 'ancient eternal super demons of malice, murder and malignity' entered their spirits and ruled. Stalin's purges killed over 30 million people. Because of World War II and the death camps, no one can really estimate how many deaths Hitler caused.

Remember, the **rejection** that is hated by the individual often becomes part of the individual. Isn't it strange that the young male growing up in a home witnessing physical abuse of his mother by his father, would always state that he would never abuse a woman. However, not only is most learning through imitation, but demon spirits are transferred to those persons in the home who are continuously exposed to the same demonic forces. By the time the child is an adult, he has witnessed social interaction at its worse – physical abuse of his mother, without learning the real meaning of love and family. His only way of responding to pain and disappointment is to abuse someone. All too often the same child who said he would never abuse a woman becomes an abuser. It is the plan of Satan that **'acts of rejection'** father more **'acts of rejection'.**

Then there are individuals, plagued and beset with alienation, frustration and **rejection,** who will often join groups that make them feel better about themselves or help them feel a sense of belonging. That can range from murderous gangs like NeoNazis, skinheads, MS-13, the Bloods and the Crips to even the church.

An interesting phenomenon happens even in the church. People want not only to belong but to be admired and/or have authority and position. Sometimes individuals, although they love God and serve God, still carrying *'the spirit of rejection'*, struggle too hard for position and power in the church.

Satan, the absolute deceiver, is a master psychologist. He will tailor his wiles and his blueprint for destruction to each person's inherited traits, family culture, and personal experience. He will, in some form or another, use pride, rebellion selfishness and **rejection. NO ONE IS EXEMPT!** As one friend said, the only good thing that can be said about Satan is than he is not prejudiced. So everyone must recognize that he /she needs help over and beyond their wealth, education, race, looks or organizational affiliation – THE PEACE OF GOD.

REJECTION 'DETHRONED' BY JESUS

*"He that committeth sin is of the devil: for the devil sinneth from the beginning. **For this purpose the SON OF GOD WAS MANIFESTED, that he might DESTROY the works of the devil"** (1 John 3:8).*

Satan was given authority to dominate in the earth by Adam; Adam disobeyed God while obeying Satan. Since then, Satan who had already been **rejected** and thrown out of heaven now had the company of man who was thrown out of The Garden of Eden. However, God's LOVE was so great for man that He gave His Son Jesus, for an acceptable sacrifice (propitiation) for man's redemption (atonement). God wanted all men to be in a personal relationship with Him.

"Therefore, when Christ came into the world, he said 'Sacrifice and offering you did not desire, but a body you prepared for me...' Then I said, 'Here I am – it is written about me in the scroll—I have come to do your will O God'. First he said, 'Sacrifices and offerings, burnt offerings and sin offerings you did not desire, nor were you pleased with them' (although the law required them to be made). Then he said, 'Here I am, I have come to do your will.' He sets aside the first to establish the second. And by that will we have been made holy through the sacrifice of the Body of Jesus Christ once for all" (Hebrews 10:5, 7-10, NIV).

Jesus, by whom all things were created, could have come to redeem man in any way. However, He wanted man to know that He understood pain, suffering, rejection, and loss. He became our High Priest and the ultimate Living Sacrifice because *'...he was in all points tempted like we are, yet without sin'* (Hebrews 4:13b). He prepared the Sacrifice, a life of perfect holiness and He offered the Sacrifice, His Body, by becoming full of our sin.

"For he hath made Him to be <u>sin for us</u>, who knew no sin; that we might be made the righteousness of God in Him" (II Corinthians 5:21).

To make sure that no one would hesitate to come to Him for Salvation, He chose to come clothed in mediocrity and insignificance. Notice in Isaiah 53 He embodied **'the role of rejection'** to prepare Himself for Calvary. This was not only to destroy Satan's power over man, but to also show man that every sin and demonic power would be destroyed by Jesus and could therefore be defeated by man (Luke 10:19; I John 4:4).

- *'He hath no form or comeliness' v.2.*
- *'There is no beauty that we should desire him' v.2.*
- *'He is despised and **rejected of men**' v.3.*
- *'A man of sorrows and acquainted with grief' v.3*
- *'He was despised and we esteemed Him not' V.3.*

Then in addition to the **rejection** He experienced, He also carried our emotional pain and suffered for our physical sickness.

- *'Surely he hath borne our griefs and carried our sorrows' V.4.*
- *'He was wounded for our transgressions' V.5*
- *'He was bruised for our iniquities' V.5.*
- *'The chastisement of our peace was upon him' V.5.*
- *'With his stripes we are healed' V.5.*
- *'He was oppressed and afflicted' V.6*

Not only did he willingly make is grave with the wicked and even the rich (V.9) but God, His father, '...*laid on him the iniquity of us ALL' (V.7)*. Furthermore, it pleased His own Father to bruise Him and allow Him so much pain and grief. His Son Jesus was the only acceptable offering for all sin (V.10).

"And ye know that he was manifested to take away our sins: and in him is no sin" (I John 3:5).

The Bible is so awesome and fascinating because there are so many overlapping and corresponding truths written by men who did not know one another, nor did they live in the same centuries. When we read in the Gospels, we find the fulfillment of so many prophecies concerning Jesus written in the Psalms and the prophetic books like Isaiah. These facts themselves could take volumes to explore. However, we are looking at the reasons for and facts of **rejection being 'dethroned'.** God, who is almighty and from everlasting to everlasting, could have dealt with **rejection** in any way He desired. However, He wanted man to know that He understood pain and loss. This He demonstrated by allowing His Son, Jesus, to leave the portals of glory and live a lifetime of discrimination and rejection and die a death of horror and rejection. Jesus 'covered all bases' destroying sin, failure and **rejection.**

Begin even with His lineage. Genealogies represent the linchpins of who we are. You will see many genealogies (called generations) in the Bible which are often repeated. If they are in the Bible, it is because God considers them important. It is extremely relevant to explore the lineage of Jesus. For in the lineage of Jesus, there are various ethnicities (non-Jewish) and evidences of sexual sins that definitely violated the Laws of God. In Spite of this, Jesus the Lamb without Blemish came to save all.

- In Matthew 1:3, Judah (Judas) had twins Phares and Zara with Tamar (Thamar). Tamar was the Widow of Er and Onan, Sons of Judah. According to the Law, Shelah, another son of Judah should have married Tamar. (The first child conceived by the brother of the deceased would have carried on the name of the deceased brother). Since Judah ignored the Law of the Levirate Marriage and did not give Shelah in Marriage to Tamar, Tamar disguised herself as a prostitute and offered herself to Judah.[15] Of this union Perez (Phares) was born and was an ancestor of Jesus. In this part of the lineage there was deceit, prostitution and incest.

- In Matthew 1:5, Salmon and Rahab were the parents of Boaz, the great grand-father of David. Rahab was a Canaanite harlot, by profession, who lived on the walls of Jericho. She protected and hid the two Israelite

---

[15] See Genesis 38:6-30

spies and consequently she and her whole family were spared when Jericho fell.[16] Obviously, no profession or nationality blocks the Grace of God.

- In Matthew 5, Ruth a gentile woman (Moabite) married Boaz, the Father of Jesse, who was the father of David. Ruth's ancestry began with the act of incest. Moab was one of Lot's sons with his oldest daughter (Genesis 19:30-37). Although the Moabites were of mixed ancestry, they worshipped Chemosh (Baal-Peor). Remember, Balaam could not curse Israel for Balak (Numbers 22:1-20), but the Moabite women seduced Israelite men into sexual immorality which cause the judgment of God against Israel (Numbers 25:1-9). Ruth, although righteous, descended from perversion. This aspect of the lineage of Jesus indicates that all sinners involved in acts of any kind of sexual immorality are not rejected by God when they repent.

- In Matthew 1:6 it cites that Solomon was born to David and *'of her that had been the wife of Urias'*. It's very striking that Bathsheba's name is not mention but Urias' (who was one of David's mighty men) is mentioned. David committed adultery with Bathsheba who became pregnant. David orchestrated the death of Uriah the Hittite in battle. That child of adultery and murder died. However David did marry Bathsheba and had Solomon who is in the lineage of Jesus. In the

---

[16] See Joshua 2:1-21; 6:17-25; Ruth 4:20; Matt. 1:4,5.

lineage of Jesus are a murderer and an adulterer, King David.

Jesus could have come down through a perfect unmarred lineage. It is obvious that, looking at the lineage of Jesus, no individual who repents will be rejected.

If you review the circumstances of Jesus' birth, it could not have been more obscure. He was born in a small town named Bethlehem in a manger or feeding crib. There was no electricity, no running water, no sterile sheets, no labor and delivery, no doctor or midwife. Likewise, there were no hotels, motels or condos available for comfort. This had to be a medically deprived delivery at its worst and poorest. Yet He was born Savior of the world, which includes kings, statesmen, the wealthy and the poor. If there were HMOs, Jesus would have been rejected because of poverty.

Since Joseph was not His biological father, He was an illegitimate child. Jesus grew up 'on the wrong side of the tracks', a town that had no social or economic importance. Even Nathanael asked *'can any good thing come out of Nazareth'* (John 1:46). He had no claim to or relationship with the current Jewish royalty, i.e., the Sanhedrin or the High Priest. Although he was well received as a young man in Nazareth, when He began His ministry, He was **rejected** twice in his own hometown.[17] Moreover, He, as a Jew, came

---

[17] Mark 6:1-6; Luke 4:28-30.

to His own people and as a whole the Jews rejected Him (John 1:11).

When He began is public ministry at the age of 30, He like so many of the 'working poor' was really homeless.

"And Jesus saith unto him, 'The foxes have holes, and the birds of the air have nests; but the Son of man hath not where to lay his head" (Matthew 8:20).

The Pharisees who perceived themselves as having final authority in regards to the law, constantly maligned Jesus (Matthew 12:24, 45) and rejected His mission and His righteousness (Luke 7:26-48). They even accused Him of having a devil.[18] Remember, for 400 years after Malachi, God did not speak through the prophets as He had in the past. During the second century BC, the Hasidim (Chasim) arose to counter the strong Hellenic influence among the Jews. Out of this group came the Pharisees. The Pharisees observed the law carefully but for the wrong reasons — to be admired of men. They became exclusive and selective and looked down on sinners. When Jesus came, He came operating differently from the Pharisees and the 'traditions of the elders'.

When Jesus fulfilled all the law and began to expose their spiritually bankrupt legalism and their godless pride and arrogance, they had to reject Him and His teaching. Despite the fact that the Pharisees, Sadducees and Scribes

---

[18] John 7:20; John 8:48, 50.

had witnessed and/or heard of the many miracles of feeding, healing and deliverance, they refused to accept Jesus as the Son of God. Not only did they reject His ministry and His deity, they wanted Him dead. Every thing leading to His crucifixion mirrored **rejection** and more **rejection.** Never once did He allow the *'spirit of rejection'* to affect Him.

- He was betrayed by Judas (Luke 47-51).
- Even though Jesus took Peter, James and John to Gethsemane to keep Him company, they slept while He prayed during the time of His agonizing prayer (Matthew 26:36-46).
- After Peter rashly cut off Malchus' ear, Jesus healed the ear. Then the soldiers arrested Him anyhow (Luke 22:50-51).
- The high priest accused Jesus of blasphemy and lying. He was spit on and struck (Matthew 26:57-67).
- Herod and his men mocked Him and scourged him (Luke23:11-16).
- Pilate, admittedly, found no wrong in Jesus and rejected Jesus in favor of the murderer Barabbas.
- During all this, His friends distanced themselves from Him (Luke 22:57-61).
- Because He became sin for us, from the sixth to the ninth hour, God separated Himself from His Son – **rejected Jesus.** The earth was in darkness, and quaked until Jesus gave up the Ghost (Matthew 20:50-53).

• Even when the evidence was given of His resurrection, the chief priest and elders paid soldiers to say the disciples had stolen His body (Matthew 28:11-15).

Never once did **rejection** by the religious leaders, the society and even His friends, effect Him or alter His mission, that is, to suffer in all points just as any human would and remain without sin, the Unblemished Lamb of God. When He arose He affirmed:

"All power is given unto me in heaven and in earth... and, lo, I am with you always, even unto the end of the world" (Matthew 28:18,20b).

That *'all power'* refers to the Power of sonship in believers.

"For it became him, for whom are all things, in bringing many sons unto glory, to make the captain of their salvation perfect through sufferings. For both HE that sanctifieth and they who are sanctified are all of one: for which cause HE is not ashamed to call them brethren" (Hebrews 2:10-11).

"For whatsoever is born of God overcometh the world: and this is the victory that overcometh the world, even our faith" (I John 5:4).

Rejection as the ruling spirit has been 'dethroned' because Jesus conquered death and ALL THE POWER OF THE ENEMY. The believer must understand that **acts of rejection** will come from family, society, institutions, coworkers, church members and enemies. However, because of the peace that surpasses understanding, these acts are just that, acts that will only affect you with the *'spirit of rejection'* if you allow it.

Rejection as the ruling spirit is dethroned because He has given the born again Holy Ghost filled believer KINGDOM AUTHORITY. 'Kingdom' is a contraction of and means king's dominion. In Genesis 1:26 God gave man and woman DOMINION over everything, which was lost when they submitted to the serpent. However Jesus came and sacrificed Himself to return to man, the born again believer, spiritual dominion in the earth. Jesus taught His followers:

Neither shall they say, Lo here, or, lo there! For behold, the kingdom of God is within you" (Luke 17:21).

That means that all believers have been given the KEYS OF THE KINGDOM, binding and loosing.

"And I will give unto thee the keys of the kingdom of heaven: and whatsoever thou shalt bind on earth shall be bound in heaven: and whatsoever thou shalt

loose on earth shall be loosed in heaven" (Matthew 16:19).

Satan has been dethroned because every believer has been granted kingdom authority to limit and stop the plans of Satan's deceptions. Unfortunately, too few believers exercise their KINGDOM AUTHORITY. However, the Word of God in the very first chapter of Revelations reminds that Jesus has washed us in His Own Blood and <u>made us kings and priests unto God</u>. Therefore Satan may be *'prince of this world'* but as kings and priests unto God, we have KINGDOM AUTHORITY over the *'prince of darkness'* (Satan). However, POWER IS NEVER POWER UNTIL IT IS RELEASED.

"Behold, I give unto you POWER to tread on serpents and scorpions, and over all the power of the enemy: and nothing shall by any means hurt you" (Luke10:19).

IDENTIFYING AND DESTROYING REJECTION'S POWER

"If the Son shall therefore make you free, ye shall be free indeed" (John 8:36).

Free people are not bound, manipulated or controlled by other persons or 'spirits' (demons) like **rejection.** *'Free'* is defined as:

1. Enjoying personal freedom, not subject to control or domination by another;
2. Choosing or capable of choosing for itself;
3. Exempt, relieved or released especially from a burdensome or noxious or deplorable condition or obligation.

'Indeed' is defined as 'without question'.

Clearly those who have not accepted Christ as their personal Savior are not free of Satan's dominion and rule. However, much less clearly are those persons who have accepted Christ and apparently are not yet completely free from satanic manipulation and power. Many continue to have spiritual deficits. *"My people are destroyed for a lack of knowledge…" (Hosea 4:6).* 'Spiritual ignorance' must be considered a demon which can be like 'a smoke screen' for **rejection.**

> *"The thief cometh not, but for to steal and to kill and destroy, but I am come that they might have life, and that they might have it more abundantly" (John 10:10).*

Robbers and thieves do not announce their plans but they subtly steal, kill and destroy as necessary. Satan's subtly works at eroding your peace (stealing), killing your joy and faith and finally destroying you spiritually. It appears that many who come to the Lord and love the Lord with all their hearts become spiritually paralyzed and ineffective – 'bound'. When a person is newly saved from their sins (born again), with his mind and will (soul) he has confessed and surrendered, and was justified (his 'slate wiped clean'). This brought him/her into fellowship (reconciled) with God because the sinful spirit was recreated (born with a new spirit). However, the mind and spirit may be new, but the old ways of thinking, feeling and acting are the things which the sanctification process must deal with.

'Spiritual ignorance' rules well when Satan oppresses the individual with old thoughts or sends temptations of the past. Sometimes individuals do not know how to fight and distinguish demonic attacks and oppression from who they really are as born again believers. In order to identify Satan's manipulation, the individual must identify the 'power of the past' which more often than not included many episodes of rejection.

The first step is recognizing who you really are. You are a composite of many things. Basically, there are three general areas.

1. You are the genetic offspring of your parents. You received 26 chromosomes which carried all the genes that determined how you would look, your height, your color, your talents and intellectual capacities, even your fat distribution.

2. You are the offspring of the 'social genetics' of your family culture. You had nothing to do with what family you were born into, nor did you decide communication patterns. You had no authority over your parents'/ guardians' parenting skills, nor parents' leisure time activities or habits, etc. All these helped to mold your personal culture.

3. Finally, you are also the result of personal experience. Personal experience includes the kind of schools and teachers responsible for your education, your personal leisure time preferences, all the support and encouragement you received from friends and family as well as all the abuse and trauma in your life.

You bring 'ALL OF YOU', that is, all of your life experiences to any relationship whether it is with God or even to the marriage. If your past is not dealt with adequately (at least with repentance and forgiveness), you will be dominated and/or manipulated by the past. Thoughts and feelings of 'the old man' will surface and immediately Satan will oppress the believer with unworthiness and guilt.

It must be understood that Jesus washes sins away but not life's experiences. Experience is imprinted in memory, some of which is on an unconscious level. **Negative experiences of the past even when** it is not remembered can and does affect current behavior. First of all, past experience will affect your personality and behavior. One young woman had many disappointments from those she trusted, especially her parents and she was also sexually abused. She now trusts no one. She has therefore become a recluse and won't even correspond with relatives.

Some experience, as bad as it is, becomes learned behavior and part of personal culture, e.g., violence begets violence. As much as a male child will hate abuse in his family, he may respond to life's frustration by abusing someone in his family. Whatever negative experiences occurred, demon spirits of rejection will always be involved. These 'spirits' should not be in the believer. However, that does not mean that the thoughts, feelings, and some times negative behavior will not follow the born again believer until he/she learns about spiritual warfare. That is the reason God placed diverse ministries in the body of Christ for the body of Christ.

> *"And he gave some, apostles; and some prophets; and some evangelists, and some, pastors and teachers; for the* **perfecting of the saints**, *for the* **work of the ministry**, *for the* **edifying of the body of Christ:** *Till we all come in the unity of the faith and of the knowledge of the Son of God, unto a perfect man, unto the measure of the stature of the fullness of Christ: That we henceforth be* **no more children**, *tossed to and fro, and carried about with the weight of every wind of doctrine, by the sleight of men, and cunning craftiness, whereby they lie in wait to deceive" (Ephesians 4:1-14)*

All believers must be constantly taught about the wiles of the enemy and trained to fight guilt, doubt and temptation.

CASE #1

I met and ministered to a young man over a period of two years. He would not look you in the eye; he kept his head down and his hands in his pocket. His main statement was 'I don't know why I can't do anything'. He was full of 'low self-esteem', 'insecurity' and 'fear'. He joined the military because he did not really have to make decisions, they could all be made for him.

He accepted the Lord while in the military; his pastor began counseling him. He had a childhood full of poverty, miseducation, rejection, and fear. Being a naturally quiet shy person with a slight build, bordering on being skinny, the tough inner city school system was a harsh frightening place for him.

His father had abandoned the family (the mother, two children) when he was quite young. His mother had to work long hard hours to support the two children with poverty wages. Knowing that these two children were timid and alone, the neighborhood children 'picked on them' so much, they remained indoors most of their childhood years.

He had no friends and soon began to feel so inferior; he began to believe he could not accomplish anything. The fear of people was worse. For example, on the day of his Junior High School graduation while riding the bus, a tough looking you man told him he liked his suit. This frightened him so much he never road the bus again. His high school was three miles from his home, rain or shine, sleet or snow, he walked to school.

Even after graduating from high school and working on a job, three youngsters approximately 10 years old, approached him for 25 cents while he was on the way to work. He ran and they chased him and were waiting for him after work. The other men in the factory had to assist him going home.

Life was so unbearable, he felt joining the service would make life better. Consequently, he joined the U.S. Military. He started attending a Church of God in Christ near his Base and accepted the Lord as his personal Savior. After the pastor counseled him and showed him that these were satanic forces of **'inferiority'**, **'low self-esteem'** and **'rejection,** informing him that these 'demon spirits' did not belong to him. As he was taught, prayed for and ministered to, those demons were eventually bound and cast out. He was filled with the Holy Ghost and 'the Mighty Burning Fire'. Everything that was not of God and was not like God was 'burned out of the inner man'. In reality according to II Corinthians 5:17, he was a new creature, because his soul was surrendered and his 'spirit' or 'inner man' became part of the Family of God.

He then took several tests and made Sergeant. He learned how to work, program and repair computers on the base so that others had to seek him out for assistance. He was able to testify, laugh and joke about himself and his past fear and inferiority. Best of all he made many new friends. For example, I requested his pastor to allow him to accompany me to a University where I was the annual spring conference speaker for Intervarsity. Not only did he mix well with the college students, he was also able to minister to several young men suffering with **rejection, fear of the future** and **fear of failure.** During the four days at the Conference, we had trouble keeping up with him because of so many new friends he was able to encourage and help.

Satan, who cannot read your mind, has a 'familiar spirit' assigned to you all the days of your life.[19] This 'spirit' is well aware of all your experiences and how each experience affected you physically, emotionally and mentally in the past. Satan and his 'demon(s)' will send the thoughts and feelings to your areas of vulnerability. Of course the oppressive thoughts or feelings and even bad dreams are accompanied with shame, guilt and /or disgust. *'He who the son has*

---

[19] Remember, Satan imitates God, God has an angel that encamps about them that fear God (Psalm 34:7). Likewise Satan has a 'demon' following each individual.

set free is free indeed' has lost relevance to the person who is bombarded with the past and does not fight.

'Indeed' refers to the fact that your thoughts and/or feeling do not determine your Salvation. When Satan keeps oppressing individuals with the past, not only is **rejection ruling,** but also **unworthiness** and **guilt.** The struggling tormented born again believer somehow does not know how to appropriate the power of the Word of God.

'There is therefore NOW no condemnation to them which are IN CHRIST JESUS, who walk not after the flesh, but after the Spirit. For by the law of the Spirit of life IN CHRIST JESUS has made me free from the law of sin and death" (Romans 8;1,2).

Rejection is supposed to be dethroned in the believer's life. However, **rejection** and it's residues of fear, anger, inferiority, etc. are not going any where until you appropriate the Power of the Word. **Agree with the Word. Pray the Word. Memorize the Word.** Place your name wherever there is a pronoun as you quote or pray the Word. As the Word becomes alive in the individual, Satan and all his oppressive forces must flee.

"Great peace have they which love thy law: and nothing shall offend them" (Psalm119:165).

"Thou wilt keep him in perfect peace, who's mind is stayed on thee: because he trusteth in thee" (Isaiah 26:3).

*"Peace, I leave with you, **my peace I give unto you**: not as the world giveth, give I unto you" (John 14:27).*

The Christian must realize that he/she has the Power to REBUKE, BIND, RENOUNCE, DISPOSSESS and CAST OUT demons of oppression from the past and present. Survival and victory involves dealing immediately and continuously with every thing that Satan sends.

"For the weapons of our warfare are not carnal, but MIGHTY through God to the pulling down of strong holds; Casting down imaginations, and every high thing that exalted itself against the knowledge of God, and bringing into captivity EVERY THOUGHT to the obedience of Christ" (II Corinthians 10:4,5).

In other words, every born again individual is equipped to deal with the past. You have been given powerfully effective weapons.

THE WORD OF GOD

"Is not MY WORD like as a FIRE? saith the Lord; and like a HAMMER that breaketh a rock to pieces?" (Jeremiah 23:29).

"He sent HIS WORD and healed them and delivered them from their destructions" (Psalm 107:20).

THE NAME OF JESUS

"In MY NAME shall they cast out devils; they shall speak with new tongues; they shall take up serpents; and if they drink any deadly thing, it shall not hurt them, they shall lay hands on the sick and they shall recover" (Mark 16:17-18).

THE BLOOD OF JESUS

"...For the accuser of our brethren is cast down, which accused them before God day and night. And they OVERCAME him by the BLOOD OF THE LAMB, and the word of their testimony; and they loved not their lives unto the death" (Revelations 12:10,11).

THE HOLY GHOST

"When the enemy shall come in like a flood, the SPIRIT OF THE LORD shall lift up a standard against him" (Isaiah 59:19).

Dealing with the past is a lot easier said than done. Satan is so shrewd he overwhelms the individual with the pain of the past – the thoughts, the dreams, the emotions, the hatred, etc. For example, how could anyone deal with experiencing their father as a sexual predator? Worse, the abused often believes that their mother knew and could have done something. It is the plan of the enemy to overwhelm individuals at younger and younger ages to warp and destroy their lives. The formula may appear difficult but it's nevertheless simple. Every individual is made in the image of God, with a will for self-determination.

"For if ye forgive men their trespasses, your heavenly Father will also forgive you: But if ye forgive not men their trespasses, neither will you father forgive your trespasses" (Mark 11:14,15).

Forgive because unforgiveness opens doorways for Satan to walk in with (in addition to the *'spirit of rejection'*) bitterness, resentment, hatred, etc. Forgiving closes the doors to the painful past. That is to say that, present behavior will NOT be manipulated by '**acts of rejection**' from the past. Every individual that truly forgives knows when total freedom is present simply because memories of the past are no longer accompanied with pain and torment.

Forgive because every bit of unforgiveness gives past offender(s) power over you. God cannot heal the pain of your memories until you forgive. Moreover, without realizing it, that person who caused all the pain and rejection is still controlling you because you do not forgive or believe you are unable to forgive. All too often, the refusal to forgive is reinforced with the 'spirit of revenge'. Really, the victim wants the abuser to experience or know what he/she is going through and has gone through. That may never happen. Yet that abuser, who may be in the grave, is still controlling areas of the victim's life when forgiveness is not forthcoming.

Get angry enough at what Satan has done to you to do whatever is necessary to be free from the bondage of the past. Freedom from a past full of **rejection** begins with **FORGIVENESS.** Forgiveness includes **forgiving yourself.** Sometimes the residue of the abuser's rage and/or filth is left with the victim and will affect similar behavior in the victim. FORGIVE YOURSELF! Or, Satan will send, in addition to everything else, 'guilt' and 'self-hatred'.

FORGIVE because no uncleanness can make it into heaven. Jesus became sin for us and forgives all sin in anyone that repents. In order to be in a right relationship with him, we must always realize there can be sins of the heart (hidden sins like hatred). Even though the believer who is carrying wounds feels like and often says, 'but I did not do anything'. Perhaps, that may be true. However, in the process of something being done to an individual, Satan deposits sins of the heart like unforgiveness, bitterness, hatred or even 'a spirit of entitlement' (that is, I am due preferential treatment because of all my suffering). The victim needs to forgive as well as repent for carrying Satan's 'baggage' in their heart.

Jesus is a merciful, tender, kindhearted Savior. He does understand how difficult forgiving can be. He will help melt your heart to the place of willingness to forgive. **God truly cares!** Once any individual prays 'God I want to forgive, I want to be free, help me to forgive', God will help that person say and mean, I forgive Lord. Joseph Scriven (1819-1886) penned this appropriate hymn.

What a friend we have in Jesus,
All our sins and griefs to bear!
What a privilege to carry
Ev'rything to God in prayer
O What peace we often forfeit,
O what needless pain be bear,
All because we do not carry
Ev'rything to God in prayer!

Always know who you are and whose you are. Satan may be 'prince of this world', but every born again believer is royalty (I Peter 2:9).

"And from Jesus Christ, who is the faithful witness, and the first-begotten of the dead, and the prince of kings of the earth. Unto him the loved us, and washed us from our sins in his own blood, and hath MADE US KINGS AND PRIESTS unto God and his Father, to him be glory and dominion for ever and ever. Amen" (Revelations 1:5,6).

Never forget the following.

1. When you are saved from you sins, you have eternal life. No one can take this from you. Only you allow failure and backslide.
2. Satan hates you because he hates Jesus and as a believer you are part of the Body of Christ (I Corinthians 12:13), as well as His ambassador (II Corinthians 5:20).

   "If the world hates you, ye know that it hated me before it hated you. If ye were of the world, the world would love his own: but because ye are not of the world, but I have chosen you out of the

world, therefore, the world hateth you" *(John 15:18,19).*

3. You have been given resurrection power and the Lord always causes you to triumph (II Corinthians 2:14).

"Ye are of God, little children, and have overcome them: because greater is he that is in you, than he that is in the world" (I John 4:4).

Strategies to Destroy 'Rejection's Power

It is Satan's job to destroy the saints. If Satan is *'prince of this world'*, he is never going to stop his attacks against you, your family, on your job, in your church, etc.

1. **Recognize that** Satan works in several areas at once. Be sure that he is always working in more than one area. If you have had to deal with **rejection** in childhood, he will send **rejection** in your marriage, on your job and even in your church. Remember, he hates the believer.

2. **Recognize that** your soul (mind) is the control center for what 'spirit of man' and body will receive and act upon. Therefore, you must always discipline your mind.

*"Finally, brethren, whatsoever things are **true**, whatsoever things are **honest**, whatsoever things are **just**, whatsoever things are **pure**, whatsoever things are **lovely**, whatsoever things of **good report**; if there be any virtue, and if there be any praise, **think on these things**" (Philippians 4:8).*

Part of disciplining your mind is refusing to have a **passive mind**. A **passive mind** is a fertile field for Satan's oppressive thoughts, subliminal or otherwise. Even watching television, in some respects, can be considered a **passive act** with **a passive mind**. In other words, even the programs you watch can affect your thoughts and desires. Therefore, there must be a constant effort to protect and discipline your mind by studying and memorize the Word of God, reading worthwhile literature, going back to school, working with people who can benefit from your skills, etc. Satan will never deceive the person who is disciplined in their walk with God.

3. **Recognize that** you will always be in 'warfare' at some level whether it is your thoughts or with rebellious children or with spiteful coworkers, etc. You must recognize that you are in charge spiritually wherever you are because God has given the believer *'all power over the power of the enemy'* (Luke 10:19).

If you do not take the 'high ground', you may soon feel overwhelmed with cares. If you ever get into a mode of loneliness, self-pity, weariness, particularly becoming over-tired, Satan will take advantage of your situation. Just as we must never fail to worship and thank God daily, likewise we must remember to pray against the wiles of the enemy daily. If you have children, never fail to pray for them every day and rebuke the plans of the enemy to destroy them. Your strategy must always include binding, rebuking, renouncing, dispossessing and casting out everything that is not of God in you, your family, your job, your church– **rejection, low self-esteem, failure, fear of failure, family disunity, despair, hopelessness, willfulness, selfishness, resentment, bitterness, hatred, murder, anger, rage, all lust, covetousness, envy, jealousy and physical and mental torment.** Furthermore, ask God to give you the discerning you need for these times, so you will know how to pray and know what strongholds to tear down. Even though Satan will never stop, he will have to know that he is defeated in your presence.

4. **Recognize that** your warfare prayers are much more powerful when you pray the Word in those prayers. When you feel alone and as though no one cares, pray, *'according to Hebrews 13:5, Lord, you said you would never leave me nor forsake, therefore I*

will be content'. When praying for a relative, pray, *'Lord, according to Luke 19:10, you came to save my relative and I thank you in advance for his/her salvation"*. Satan will often attempt to bring doubt and fear, pray, *'According to II Timothy 1:7, I receive your power in me and a sound mind from you'*. When plagued with lusts of any kind, pray, *'According to Romans 6:6 and Galatians 2:20 my sinful nature has been crucified and I will not serve sin'*.

5. **Recognize that** Satan will attempt to diminish your faith with family struggles and sins making you believe that your family is under some kind of curse. That is just **rejection** in another form. Pray against any behavior or 'demons' that appears to be too prevalent in your family. Sometimes there are demonic assignments passed down through generations to destroy families. Pray everyday if necessary, *'I take authority and separate any and all curses assigned to me or my family. I break all generational curses by the Blood of Jesus and I stand in the gap for my family. In the Name of Jesus, I receive every blessing that Christ has given me and I agree with His Word which states, "Blessed be the God and Father of our Lord Jesus Christ who hath blessed us with all spiritual blessings in heavenly places in Christ..." (Ephesians 1:2)*.

6. **Recognize that** you can wear Satan down. When he is relentless in his attacks, get Bible tapes. Play

them in your home, in your car, even very softly on your job. Play them when going to bed and when you awaken. If Satan torments you in your sleep, wake up and read the Bible aloud, particularly **Revelations 20:10.** Satan and his demons hate the Word of God, particularly the Book of Revelations.

A mighty fortress is our God,
A bulwark never failing:
Our helper he amid the flood
Of mortal ills prevailing.
For still our ancient foe
Doth seek to work us woe
His craft and pow'r are great,
And, armed with cruel hate,
On earth is not his equal.

Did we our strength confide,
Our striving would be losing
Were not the right Man on our side,
The Man of God's own choosing.
Dost ask who that my be?
Christ Jesus, *it is He-*
Lord Sabaoth His name,
From age to Age the same-
And He must win the battle.
(Martin Luther, 1483 -1546)

7. **Recognized that** personal sanctification is an absolute for all believers. Each person must not only discipline their thoughts but work on shedding past behaviors that can limit or hinder the sanctification process. For example, if a person has been saved and freed from intermittent or chronic depression, that person must work on behavior associated with depression. Remember depression is a 'spirit' associated with rejection. Therefore, if isolation was the norm, that person must work at being involved with people.

I ministered to a young woman, that was chronically depressed, preferring to be alone most of time. The Lord truly saved and delivered her. However, she could not bring herself to become consistently involved in church activities (preferring always to be alone) and that same 'spirit of depression' again overtook her.

Isaiah 61:3 states that God gives the *'garment of praise for the spirit of heaviness'*. You 'put on praise' and 'give the sacrifice of praise' by the act of your will. Putting on 'a garment of praise' means that you are shedding or putting off the 'spirit of depression'. This concept of changing behavior as part of the sanctification process is one of the tools to prevent Satan having any victory over you. Remember, this will have to include unacceptable leisure time activities also. The *'very God of peace'* will sanctify you wholly when you have done all you can do to distance yourself from the control of Satan and the world (I Thessalonians 5:23).

8. **Recognize that** you need at least one confidant. After you have done all you need to do to prevent **rejection** from affecting you and the **spirit of rejection** from controlling you, you still need to talk. When an individual talks about past pain, healing and deliverance is concretized. When you talk about pain and forgiveness, you are letting Satan know that the filth, mistreatment and pain is not a part of you and will not affect your behavior. Remember, God created psychotherapy. *"Confess your faults **one to another,** and pray **one for another**, that ye may be healed..." (James 5:16).*

9. Finally, every individual needs to **recognize** those areas of vulnerability in their life. There will be times that individuals are so busy, they are not watchful and prayerful.

*"**And the cares of this world**, the deceitfulness of riches, and the lusts of other things entering in, choke the Word and it becometh unfruitful" (Mark 4:19).*

CASE # 3
LOSING GROUND

This young man grew up in a violent family, receiving more physical abuse than love. He dropped out of school at the age of 10 years old and never able to get a decent job began a life of crime and doing jail time in many prisons. **Rejection** was added to more **rejection. Rejection** opened him up to demons of revenge, anger and rage. After much violence even against his wife, he came to the church and accepted the Lord. God blessed him to get an excellent job and he worked very hard as a soul winner particularly in the prisons.

Satan is shrewd. All of the things this young man never had, he was able to purchase with 'plastic money' – credit cards. He became so overwhelmed with debt, he began working more and more, staying out of church and neglecting the ministry. Since he had been so violent, he was warned never to place himself in the place of violence. But Satan knew the point in which he was most vulnerable. When he discovered the person who had stolen something from him, **'Rage'** returned and caused him to almost kill a man with a bat. His shame and the **'spirit of rejection'** really began to rule, he began staying away from the church, eventually backsliding and subsequently divorcing and losing his family.

*"For they that are after the flesh do mind the things of the flesh, but they that are after the Spirit the things of the Spirit. For to be carnally minded is death; but to be spiritually minded is **life and peace"** (Romans 8:5,6).*

Keeping your relationship with the Master is not difficult once the individual decides nothing is more important than having the PEACE OF GOD and ETERNAL LIFE.

CONCLUSION
I AM WHO THE WORD OF
GOD SAYS THAT I AM!!!

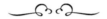

The Bible is the current and final authority on salvation including eternal life. Satan wants to weaken faith and commitment and ultimately precipitate failure in believers. The hope of the believer rests in God and His Word. Our job is to 'rest' in God, His Promises and His Peace. Remember, *"There hath no temptation taken you but such as is common to man: but God is faithful, who will not suffer you to be tempted above that ye are able; but will with temptation ALSO make a way to escape that ye may be able to bear it"* (*I Corinthian 10:13*). We can only know this by knowing His Word and appropriating the Power of His Word. Reading the Word, Meditating on His Word, Memorizing His Word and Studying His Word are all tools to appropriate the Power in and of His Word.

When the Word becomes an integral power of your thought life and your faith, you have begun to empower yourself with His Glory. Speak life and Power to yourself!

I AM A NEW CREATURE and the past has no control over my present or future.

> *"Therefore, if any man be in Christ, he is a new creature, **OLD THINGS ARE PASSED AWAY**, behold, all things are become new" (II Corinthians 5:17).*

I AM NOT REJECTED because I am a child of God and therefore part of a huge loving family, THE FAMILY OF GOD.

> *"The Spirit itself beareth witness with our spirit, that we are the children of God: and if children, then heirs, heirs of God and joint heirs with Christ" (Romans 8:16-17).*

I AM LOVED. Since by definition God is Love, then all the empty places where there is *'the lack of love'*, God gives a Baptism of love. Genuine parental love, sibling love, neighborly love, spousal love and come from God. Therefore God will and can fill all void and heal the pain of lost love.

"Beloved, let us love one another; for love is of God; and everyone that loveth is born of God, and knoweth God. He that loveth not knoweth not God" *(I John 4:7,8).*

"That he [Jesus Christ]would grant you according to the riches of his Glory, to be strengthened with might by his Spirit in the inner man; That Christ may DWELL in your hearts by faith; that ye being rooted and grounded in LOVE, may be able to compre-hend with all saints what is the breadth, and length, and depth, and height; ***and to know the LOVE OF CHRIST, which passeth knowledge, that ye might be filled with all the fullness of God"*** *(Ephesian 3:16-19).*

I AM STRONG because I have a personal relationship with God.

"The people that ***know their God shall be strong*** *and do exploits" (Daniel 11:32).*

"That he would grant you according to the riches of his glory, to be strengthened with might by his Spirit in the inner man" (Ephesians 3:16)

I AM MORE THAN A CONQUEROR because I am part of the body of Christ; *"For by one Spirit we are all baptized into one body, whether we be Jews or Gentiles, whether we be bond or free have been all made to drink into one Spirit" (I Corinthians 12:13).* As joint heirs with Christ (Romans 8:17), we inherit and lay claim to the power of Christ's Resurrection when He destroyed ALL principalities and powers.

"In all these things I am **MORE THAN A CONQUEROR** *through him that loved us" (Romans 8:37).*

I AM DAILY OVERCOMING THE DEVIL because of who I am in Christ and Who Christ is in me.

"Ye are of God little children, **and have overcome them***: because GREATER is HE that is in you, than he that is in the world" (I John 4:4).*

"And they **overcame him** *by the BLOOD OF THE LAMB and THE WORD OF THEIR TESTIMONY; and they loved not their lives unto the death" (Revelations 12:11).*

I AM EXERCISING MY AUTHORITY OVER THE ENEMY because Satan will never stop sending trouble, trials and temptation. Therefore, I relentlessly use the POWER that Jesus has freely given me over Satan.

"Behold, I give unto you POWER to tread on serpents and scorpions, and over all the power of the enemy; and nothing shall by any means hurt you" (Luke 10:19).

I AM WORTHY OF MINISTRY because the Spirit of God in me has made me worthy to continue the work of Christ.

"Now then we are ambassadors for Christ. . . For he hath made him to be sin for us, who knew no sin; that we might be made the righteousness of God in him" (II Corinthians 5:20-21).

I AM FREE OF ALL MENTAL TORMENT because I choose to keep my mind stayed on the Lord.

"Thou will keep him in perfect peace, whose mind is stayed on thee: because he trusteth in thee" (Isaiah 26:3).

I DAILY DISCIPLINE MY THOUGHT LIFE AND MY LEISURE TIME ACTIVITIES because God has given me a will plus His POWER.

*"Finally, brethren, whatsoever things are **true,** whatsoever things are **honest,** whatsoever things are **just,** whatsoever things are **pure,** whatsoever things are **lovely,** whatsoever things are of **a good report;** if there be any virtue, if there be any praise, **THINK ON THESE THINGS"** (Philippians 4:8).*

*"For the weapons of our warfare are not carnal, but **mighty through God** to the pulling down of strongholds; **casting down imaginations** and every high thing that exalteth itself against the knowledge of God, and **BRINGING INTO CAPTIVITY EVERY THOUGHT TO THE OBEDIENCE OF CHRIST...**" (II Corinthians 10:4-5).*

I AM NOT AFRAID because fear is faith in what Satan can do and I refuse to place faith in Satan. Fear can only remain if I allow it to remain.

*"For God hath not given me the spirit of fear but POWER, LOVE and A **SOUND MIND"** (II Timothy 1:7)*

"When thou liest down, thou shalt not be afraid: yea, thou shalt lie down, and thy sleep shall be sweet. Be not afraid of sudden fear, neither of the desolation of the wicked, when it cometh. For the Lord shall be thy

confidence, and shall keep thy foot from being taken"
(Proverbs 3:24-26).

*". . .**Fear not,** I have redeemed thee, I have called*
thee by thy name; thou art mine. When thou passest
through the waters, I will be with thee; and through
the rivers, they shall not overthrow thee: when thou
walkest through the fire, thou shalt not be burned;
neither shall the flame kindle upon thee" Isaiah
43:1-2).

I AM KEPT IN SAFETY WHEREVER I GO because
God is with me wherever I go.

"Lo, I am with you always, even unto the end of the
world" (Matthew 28:20). "For he shall give his
angels charge over thee, to keep thee in all thy ways"
(Psalm 91:11).

Knowing God, knowing his promises, and relying on His
protection, is knowing how to REST IN GOD. That is to say
that knowing when things do not appear to be fair or right, it
is nevertheless all right. The Christian's problems are God's
problems. The Christian's concerns are God's concerns.
Therefore, casting all care to Him according I Peter 5:7 is an
act of confidence and faith. Included in those cares are **'acts**

of rejection' from people, relatives or coworkers as well as the pain that attends the acts.

The Word of God has to be every Christian's lifeline and source. *"Seek ye out of the book of the Lord, and read: no one of these shall fail. . ." (Isaiah 34:16).* As long as each person is alive, Satan, 'the prince of this world' and 'the prince of the powers of the air' has legions of demons whose main job is to destroy men everywhere. He has no power over any child of God who is 'rooted and grounded' in the Word of God. Jesus is the Word made flesh. Therefore, the Word (Jesus) received and the Word studied (the scriptures) is an immediate and everlasting certainty. Therefore all Christians can defeat the eternally rejected one, Satan, by rejecting **in the Name of Jesus, with the Word of God, with Blood of Jesus and the Holy Spirit** all the REJECTION Satan sends.

"Now, brethren, I commend you to God, and to the word of His Grace, which is able to build you up and to give you an inheritance among all them which are sanctified" (Acts 20:32).

BIBLIOGRAPHY

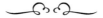

THE HOLY BIBLE, King James Version

THE HOLY BIBLE, New International Version

Rebecca Brown

    HE CAME TO SET THE CAPTIVES FREE

Fay Ellis Butler

    AFTER DELIVERANCE, THEN WHAT?

    CALLED TO SAINTS

    CALLED BE WARRIORS

    HOW TO MINISTER TO THE SEXUALLY ABUSED

Oliver C. Cox

    CASTE, CLASS AND RACE

Marable Manning

    HOW CAPITALISM underdeveloped BLACK
    AMERICA

Daniel P. Mannix and Malcolm Cowley

    BLACK CARGOES: A History of the Atlantic Slave
    Trade

Watchman Nee

THE SPIRITUAL MAN

Ordover, Nancy

American Eugenics: Race, Queer Anatomy, The Science
Of Nationalism (Univ. of Minnesota Press) 2003

Jesse Penn-Lewis

WAR AGAINST THE SAINTS

Derek Prince

BLESSINGS OR CURSES

Walter Rodney

HOW EUROPE UNDERDEVELOPED AFRICA

Corrie Ten Boom

THE HIDING PLACE

TRAMP FOR THE LORD

OTHER BOOKS BY THE AUTHOR

After Deliverance, Then What?

Called To Be Saints

Called To Be Warriors

How to Minister to Christians in Bondage

How to Minister to The Sexually Abused

The Holy Spirit: Don't Live Here or Leave Here Without Him

Why Our Children Must Be Warriors

Why Pray?